How to Stop Hate Crime

My Guide to Engage Police & City Officials to Quell the Violence

Jack Castiglione

How to Stop Hate Crime is a work of nonfiction.
Some names and identifying details have been changed.

ISBN 978-1-7357062-3-8

Printed in the United States of America
Cover design by Jack Castiglione
For more information:
YouTube.com/c/JacksGayChats (Jack's Gay Chats)
JackCastiglione.com
Email: Jack.Author@outlook.com

A Letter from President Obama

June 23, 2017

Jack Castiglione
Long Beach, California

Dear Jack:

Thank you for writing. Like you, I'm proud of the many milestones America has achieved on the path toward LGBT equality. We've seen more progress made and more hearts and minds change than many ever thought possible. And those gains aren't just the result of policies – They're the result of countless acts of courage and quiet heroism spanning generations of our citizens.

Still, a lot of work remains to defend this progress and to make sure that the full promise of America extends to all our people. The task of bridging our founding creed with the realities of our time doesn't rest on any one person. It rests with all of us. Our journey as a nation depends, as it always has, on the collective and persistent effort of people like you – compassionate, caring, and open-minded – who stand up and speak out in defense of the notion that love is love and that all of us, no matter who we are or who we love, are worthy of equal dignity, equal respect, and equal protection under the law.

That's the vision for America that Michelle and I share. And I want you to know we will continue standing alongside you. Thank you, again, for writing. I wish you the very best.

Sincerely,
Barack Obama

Contents

Chapter 1:My Approach to Strategy 1

Chapter 2: You're in a Conservative State: Maybe Not the Issue ...3

Chapter 3: Approach #1 When the Chief of Police is Responsive...9

Chapter 4: Encouraging Victims to Report Hate Crime 14

Chapter 5: Assembling a Task Force 15

Chapter 6: Establish a Hate Crime Reporting Hotline 17

Chapter 7: Approach #2 When the
Chief of Police is non-Responsive 21

Chapter 8: Approach #3 When the
City Manager is non-Responsive 23

Chapter 9: Approach #4 When the
City Council is non-Responsive..............................26

Chapter 10: Approach #5 Community Meetings 28

Chapter 11: Approach #6 Civilian patrols.............................33

Chapter 12: Approach #7 What If Nothing Works 35

Chapter 13: Approach #8 Police Complaint Commission 37

Conclusions 39

Acknowledgments..40

References 41

About the Author...43

CHAPTER 1

My Approach to Strategy

The purpose of this "handbook" is not to instruct you on how to pursue your assailant, nab him, and drag him off to jail. Rather, it's to show how to get your local police officers to do it for you, as they are supposed to do. In many cities, the local police are simply not doing their job, and it is often intentional when some officers avoid serving and protecting members of the LBGTQ community.

I have worked, formally and informally, as the liaison between the Long Beach, CA, LGBTQ community and our Police Department for nearly two decades. I can tell you from my experience that almost all these officers are hard-working, honest, and dedicated people with no bias in carrying out their duties. I am proud to have been associated with the Long Beach Police Department as I helped to improve it. However, some officers in various cities do not apply the law and police procedures equally to all people. Depending on where you live, you, too, may have a huge problem in being treated fairly and attaining social justice.

The methodology I (and other community leaders) used to address and solve issues related to hate crime in the City of Long Beach can be applied throughout the United States and many cities in other countries. The exact approach you take will depend on what roadblock police and city officials put up against advancing equality and social justice for all minority groups. Where there is more acceptance, the task is quite direct and simple. However, the task will be more complex and challenging if there is less acceptance.

The path to improving police policy requires a different approach for different jurisdictions. I will address those approaches individually.

Some of you may be thinking that this book is supposed to be about stopping hate crimes, then immediately, the author brings up police policy. CORRECT! If police properly pursued and captured hate crime assailants, hate crime would be dramatically reduced, if not eliminated. Spoiler alert: There are not that many actual perpetrators of these crimes, and the problem is largely solved when they are removed from the street. Sound overly optimistic? It's not. (See Chapter 7 for details.)

CHAPTER 2

You're in a Conservative State: Maybe Not the Issue

Many people think that trying to work for equality in red states (conservative states) is hopeless because these states largely offer no support for LGBTQ equality. There is nothing to work with. It is a waste of time. Here is the good news. In major cities, even in red states, LGBTQ equality is recognized and even fully supported by city governments. In most cases, it took constant hard work to achieve improved policing. Here is one example of how a conservative state can have cities that support LGBTQ rights.

Arizona, a Mostly Red State

Arizona currently offers no state-wide protections for the LGBTQ community. Waiting for that to change… well, it may not happen until hell freezes over. Even if the state government does not act to protect members of the LGBTQ community, major cities in Arizona have enacted protective laws to varying degrees. A study of cities was completed in 2020 by the Human Rights Campaign Foundation and the Equality Federation Institute. Cities were judged based on:

- Non-discrimination laws (housing, employment, healthcare, etc.).
- Municipal-employee spousal benefits.
- Anti-bullying policies and city involvement with the LGBT community.
- Law enforcement involvement with the LGBT community.
- Leadership on LGBT equality, such as LGBT people in leadership roles.

Here are the larger Arizona cities and how they fared. The cities in Arizona which offer 100% protection for its LGBTQ people are Phoenix, Tempe, and Tucson. This is fabulous. The percentage level of protection in some other cities is quite good but should be increased. These are Flagstaff- 67%, Scottsdale- 65%, and Glendale- 63%. Chandler- 61%, and Mesa- 60%. Other cities did not fare so well, such as Peoria- 26, Gilbert- 19%, and Avondale- 15%. In this book, we are concerned about cities. We will work with cities, not states. This makes our endeavor easier.

In general, larger cities, regardless of which state they are in, already have dedicated personnel working hard and continuously to sustain and grow full equality for the LGBTQ community. Thank you! This book is intended to help people who live in medium to small cities work with their police departments and other city officials to create or improve the conduct of police officers. We need our police officers to protect and defend ALL OF US, regardless of which minority group we identify with.

This book is based on my successful experience in dramatically reducing violence in the LGBTQ community of Long Beach, California, a city of nearly half a million people. Although the issue of violence against the LGBTQ community in each locality varies greatly, the structure of municipal governments and police departments are very similar, at least concerning my approach to City Managers/Mayors, councils, and police departments. In jurisdictions covered by county government, there is always a Sheriff's facility nearby and a commander of that office similar to a Chief of Police. I will refer to the county commander of a sheriff's station as a Chief of Police.

The methodology presented to stop hate crime in LGBTQ communities around the country can also be applied to other minority groups to halt hate crimes against them, including Jews, Blacks, Asians, and others.

It must be noted that a special circumstance or hurdle hinders hate-crime solving in the gay community that does not exist in other minority groups who are often the subject of hate crimes. The fact that many gay men are closeted in their lifestyle and choose never to have their homosexuality discovered, at least not publicly, makes them highly resistant to reporting any crime against them, which would include disclosing the fact that they were in, or just left, a gay bar, or were present at any other place or event of the LGBTQ community. For our purposes, it's not important to go into why some people are closeted except to say they might feel generally embarrassed or perhaps they would be caught living a double life if they were known to be homosexual. Perhaps they feel their job would be jeopardized if their sexual orientation came to light. School teachers are one obvious job security example. Coming out and being proud of who you are is important, but it is not a subject of this book. Another reason for not reporting a hate crime is that many gay men feel it would be a waste of time because the police will not do anything. There can also be a substantial distrust of the police. So we have to work with this issue also, and we will.

All of these various reasons discourage victims from reporting hate crimes. However, we must find a way which encourages victims to report these horrible events.

In the City of Long Beach, at the time I began my police relation work, the LGBTQ community did not respect police officers, and therefore victims refused to report the crimes against them. I created the LGBTQ's Hate Crime Reporting Hotline so they could at least report the crimes to me. I personally took these reports to the Chief of Police. In other words, I acted as the gay community and police department liaison. It worked exceptionally well as a temporary fix until I could help to repair and improve the issue of police misconduct. (*The Chartreuse Garden*, shown in the list of references, describes my approach to training cadets at the Long Beach Police Academy on LGBTQ issues.)

In the mid to late 1980s, I was the only one who worked on police issues. I was part of an unofficial citizens' task force assembled to handle a wide variety of LGBTQ issues and services, from AIDS programs, counseling, rap groups, civil rights, Pride events, senior programs, and so on.

An important advantage of forming a task force is to apply political pressure to stop the violence. This same group can come together to tackle other LGBTQ issues and expand judicial justice and equal rights for our community as additional projects appear in the future.

There is a caveat I need to mention: while I worked on these anti-violence issues in Long Beach from 1975 to 1992 and was largely successful in stopping hate crimes, other community leaders had worked tirelessly in the 1960s and 1970s against this violence. Although they set up the hugely important groundwork, these heroes were unsuccessful in stopping the violence. Why? The short answer is that the city officials (meaning the City Council members) and the Chief of Police were not interested in gay rights at that time. The gay community spoke out loud, but we did not have the political power we have today. I'll address this later. (When I use the term "gay rights" or "gay community," I mean these as all-inclusive terms, which include lesbians, bisexuals, transgender people, etc. It was just the common term used at the time.)

I must also mention that although when we think of the LGBTQ community, we see our members as roughly equally divided between men and women. However, in my experience, women have done much more of the heavy lifting. They did this not only in the initial groundbreaking of the gay rights movement but in the continuing struggle for LGBTQ equality. We all owe a tremendous thank you for the role the women played and continue to play in our struggle for equality.

I need to point out that when I refer to stopping violence in Long Beach, I am solely using my hotline information to judge the enormous reduction in these crimes, which actually brought the reported assault cases I monitored to zero by 1992. This data was a small sample. But the Hate Crime Reporting Line I established in 1986 and operated for six years was consistently advertised city-wide in LGBTQ-frequented places such as discos, cafes, and bars, as well as at the gay and lesbian center and Pride events. (See Chapter 6 for more about hotlines.)

In using the methodology I am proposing, it is not important to analyze and understand why some people hate members of particular groups except to acknowledge that hatred is a learned behavior, usually in childhood and perpetuated by familial beliefs, religious organizations, and political groups.

This hatred or learned behavior is why working to re-educate children and adults is an important step in attaining equality and social justice. Stop the misinformation, and you stop the rejection. Stop the rejection, and you will stop the violence, at least substantially. But I'll leave that task to people smarter than me. However, we'll let the police and justice system re-educate criminals by imprisoning them.

Most of us understand that in our conservative states, such as the south and upper midwest, most state governments are blatantly opposed to LGBTQ rights. It would be hugely helpful if they weren't. Working on the state level to create state-wide LGBTQ protections is better left to the major civil rights groups designed to do that. And we need to support their efforts.

However, we don't need state-level cooperation or approval for our purposes. Hate crimes exist in our cities; let's deal with them on the city level. I have separated the "how-to" steps into levels of existing acceptance and have already attained equality for the LGBTQ (or whichever minority group you are in). Yes, there are! As I mentioned, we don't need to work with states; we work with cities.

As shown above, Flagstaff, Scottsdale, Glendale, Chandler, Mesa, Peoria, Gilbert, and Avondale all have some level of support for the LGBTQ community, somewhere between 60% and 10%. In these cities, you have approachable people. It's a start. Take what you have and build it up.

Our job is to stop those acting out. And we can do that locally. We can work to develop a more effective policing policy that will result in the arrest, conviction, and confinement of the individual perpetrators. This is the most effective and instant way to gain results and lower hate crime.

You're thinking, "Police already do this." Not necessarily. Not fully. Some officers do not arrest perpetrators of LGBTQ hate crimes, even though many say they do or try to. I will explain this in the next chapter.

The second point is even more shocking. Although there are millions of loud, angry voices spewing hate, and in that sense, promoting violence, VERY FEW individuals actually engage in physical assaults. My data from the six years I operated the hotline showed that when you take the few bad actors, those who commit assaults and murders, off the street, violence decreases dramatically. There is a constant supply of angry noise makers but a relatively few actual violent actors.

Before we get into the mechanics of what we need to do, let me explain that there are several levels of government we can approach to voice our grievances and work with to attain results. The one you choose depends on the type of issue that is problematic in your city. Of course, you may be dealing with multiple problems and problems on different levels requiring different approaches. Let's take them one at a time.

CHAPTER 3

Approach #1
When the Chief of Police is Responsive

Let's say, for example, an assault takes place outside of a gay bar. Let's pick the most common assault. A patron was followed from the bar (often at closing time) to his car or followed by the would-be assailant as he was walking home. The patron is attacked and beaten. He may call the police then or when he gets home, or someone else who saw the attack may make that call.

Let's say an officer arrives at the scene of the assault and briefly interviews the victim but does not take a report. The officer can give a few reasons, such as, "Well, your assailant's gone now; not much we can do." Or, "You were probably soliciting him in the bar, so he got angry and beat you up. Next time, don't go propositioning guys in bars." Meaning you got what you deserved. Or the officers can go as far as, "Look, you were committing a crime yourself by soliciting sex. I will not arrest you this time, but stop hitting on guys." In any case, the officer got out of doing a lot of report-taking paperwork. Often officers will assume a victim like this is a gay man and, therefore, will be ashamed and closeted. He assumes the victim would be too embarrassed to file a complaint against the officer. So the officer justifies not taking the crime report.

When I found out about a case where officers refused or avoided doing their duty, I wrote a letter (no emails!) and sent it to the Chief of police. Hand delivering it is even better. How do I know what officer to report? I don't need to. My letter would include information as such:

".... On September 3, at 2:20 am, an officer was called to Broadway Avenue and Falcon Street, which was a gay-bashing scene. After interviewing the victim, Thomas Jones, the officer did not take a crime report. Please look into this and send an officer to xxx address to take that man's report of this assault...."

The police department, of course, has detailed records of which officer was dispatched to answer which calls. The police dispatch logs contain the name of the responding officer. In a police department where the standard protocol is followed, that officer would then face disciplinary action, which might be a simple notation in his personnel files. Or they might have to attend a special training course, or he might be fired if he has a record of misconduct. (When I use the word "misconduct," I mean it to include ambivalence and even laziness.)

An important issue arises if the assaulted member of the LGBTQ community does not like or trust the police department. What I mean here is that some people think that if they report a crime, something bad might come back to them. Or, maybe the police will not be discreet in receiving my report. Certainly, many gays and lesbians in many cities just don't want to deal with the police for any reason. Then what? Then these crimes go unreported. It means that they never happened, and LGBTQ community leaders are bitching for nothing when they scream about improper police behavior. It is a common problem, and it was true in Long Beach in the 1960s, 1970s, and 1980s. (More details: Ref #1)

What I did was install a special hotline phone line in my home. I asked for and received approval from the board of directors of the gay and lesbian center to start the hotline. Even though I did this entirely on my own (installing the extra phone line, paying for it, advertising it, writing articles, and giving speeches about it), I wanted this hotline to have credibility. I needed the official blessing of the board of directors and the respect of the gay community at large. I was readily accepted to monitor this hotline because I had a few years of experience working with the police in my position as Chairman of the Police Relations Committee of the Long Beach Democratic Club, a background as a student of psychology, and I was available since I worked from my home. Both the gay community and the Chief of Police respected me, which made for a fabulous and productive working relationship.

In the example above, a gay person who was assaulted might not report it to the police. Back then, in Long Beach, they likely would not. The general sentiment was, "Why bother? The police won't do anything," so they would call the hotline, the Hate Crimes Reporting Line, to be exact. Psychologically speaking, it would make them feel better to do "something," and I would send or deliver the letter mentioned above to the Chief.

You won't likely be as fortunate as I was in setting up a one-on-one relationship with your Chief of Police as I was with Long Beach Chief of Police Lawrence Binkley (from 1987 to 1992). You will likely work with one of the Chief's command staff or the public relations officer. This connection will only be real and productive if the Chief supports your efforts to work on improving community policing issues. (More on the hotline in Chapter 6)

The Dreaded Department of Internal Affairs

On rare occasions, we may find ourselves confronting a police officer who is rude or ambivalent about the issue we are raising. Maybe he comes across as arrogant or outright anti-gay. He may be a rogue officer or new to the force and has not learned that he is the public servant, not the complainant. Almost all of us would think it a waste of time and energy to report the officer's unacceptable behavior. "They aren't going to do anything," I often hear. Think about it. You're just one person, and that officer is part of a huge and well-organized department of "brothers" looking out for each other. Besides, it's your word against a well-trained officer who has sworn to serve and protect. So it will do no good to make a complaint. Right?

WRONG! All charges of misconduct or misbehavior are investigated. Even if the detective of IA (Internal Affairs) finds no solid bases for discipline, the very least they do is make a note in the officer's personnel file to record this complaint. What do you think happens when a few, maybe only two other people step forward and make a similar complaint over the following months? He now has a history. Your type of charge has been reinforced by others. Your seemingly useless mention of his misconduct became part of his record. It will remain there forever. The Chief of Police will take action by either re-training the officer or outright firing him. Yes, the office of Internal Affairs is, indeed, dreaded by the rank-and-file officers.

When to Raise the Issue

Must there be a rash of gay bashings to justify a call to action to stop it? No. One act of violence must compel us to express our outrage. One act of police misconduct, such as an officer's refusal to take a crime report, must move us to find out why. One incident, and we must bring the matter to the attention of the leadership of the police department, allow them to respond, and correct the problem. The iceberg analogy (that 90% of an iceberg is underwater and therefore not seen) is appropriate. Whatever infrequent problems you see concerning LGBTQ violence, there are many more unseen incidences. The rare occurrence of an officer failing to take a crime report can be a sign that there is a hidden culture of this kind of police misconduct. Act at the first sight of a problematic issue. If the police leadership does not properly address your concern, take it to the next level, as I outline in this book.

Training Police Officers

In all larger police departments, as in larger companies, you'll find a program called "In-Service Training," or something like that. As officers work in their departments, things change over the years. Employees, in this case, police officers, need to be updated on new laws or new police procedures and practices that are being implemented.

This training session is an excellent vehicle to introduce and educate officers on new requirements and concepts in policing. Regarding introducing police officers to specific issues involving the LGBTQ community, a qualified community member would be asked to lead the session. After observing my predecessor, a psychologist who was gay, conduct a couple of these annual "gay sensitivity training sessions," I was asked to take on this volunteer job regularly. Since these were officers who had been in the force for years, they were not so interested in learning new things. The course was mandatory, but their attentiveness was not. Most seemed so bored.

It was a much different experience and more interesting assignment when I was asked to be an official instructor at the Long Beach Police Academy. These were people who would become applicants for police officer positions in Long Beach and other cities. They chose to sign up for this 9-month school because earning a certificate of completion would improve their chances of being hired anywhere. I played a small but important role in one of the classes called "The Diverse Community."

The academy class would enroll about 70 to 120 attendees each year. I would come into their class and have them for a full day, conducting it more like a discussion group rather than a lecture. These students were all ears and expressed great interest in finding out how gay and lesbian people were treated and how the community perceived the police. I even brought in recent victims of gay bashing to not only talk about their assault but, more importantly, how the attending officers treated them. My class was a huge eye-opener for most of these eager-to-learn students. (More details: Ref #2)

CHAPTER 4

Encouraging Victims to Report Hate Crime

Problems can't be solved if no one knows they exist. A hate crime committed and not reported never happened. Non-reported hate crimes can prompt some to defensively say, "Gay bashing? What gay bashing?"

Maybe you do not need a hotline to report hate crimes. However, there are four reasons you might. First, LGBTQ people tend not to report a hate crime because they are closeted. Reporting a crime might entail disclosing that it happened while exiting a gay bar or attending a gay pride festival. He has to "out" himself in the process of making the police report.

Second, although the victim sees the police department as officers doing their jobs well and fairly, the victim just does not like or trust the police, so no hate crime report is sought.

Third, even though the victim has no grudge against the police, they think the crime, which may be a simple punch, is not a big deal and not worth all the trouble to report. The victim is thinking only about his one incident and not considering that getting punched in the face is an assault frequently repeated against LGBTQ people and is a community-wide problem.

Finally, it may be a simple fact that police attitudes and common practices in your city have homophobic undertones. Some officers will outright refuse to assist any member of the LGBTQ community simply based on their personal beliefs that all gays are sexual deviants who get assaulted because they are soliciting straight men.

Therefore, establishing a hotline may be a critical piece of the puzzle in solving hate crimes, but hold on, not yet.

CHAPTER 5

Assembling a Task Force

Before we talk about specific tactics to address policing issues, let me discuss the leadership arm of the LGBQ community (or of whatever minority group you are concerned about). A task force needs to be assembled to lead this work and present the image that the LGBTQ community is highly organized. A group of leaders (call this group whatever you wish), but I suggest they come together and strategize a plan of action. I offer the acronym FACE as the face of your community which stands for Friends to Attain Community Equality.

These are people you already know. It need not be large. It can be as few as five or six people. Commonly, members of such a task force are people on your governing board representing your community, such as public figures who are outspoken proponents of your cause, someone talented in writing articles, and an LGBTQ business owner or two who would do nicely. Of these members, choose one to be the liaison with the police department as well as with city hall. They can be two different people or the same person.

I need to caution you that this kind of activism is delicate. There is no place for angry hot heads. You'll be quickly ushered out of the discussion room if they are present. Do not think of the Chief of Police, City Manager, department heads, councilpersons, or other city officials as enemies. Think of them as partners. Most likely, they want to do the right thing. Your task is to present your policing issues rationally and maybe emotionally. Yes, hate crimes such as gay bashing are an emotional issue. Express your emotional feelings when you discuss them. Many city officials, including the Chief of Police and their command staff, who are straight, have no idea how we are discriminated against. If we do not find a way to report these assaults, these offices will not understand how frequently they occur.

When I asked for a meeting with the command staff of the police department or maybe with the City Manager, I'd bring a person with me who had been recently beaten. The bruises on that person's face speak volumes. I also bring written reports and other evidence that I have taken over the hotline of similar recent assaults. When I finished presenting my case to identify the harmful effects of police misconduct, the city officials I am addressing understood the brutal disasters that commonly happen in our community. (More details: Ref #1 and #2)

Two or three members of your FACE Task Force should be present. Under the scenario I set up here, where the Chief is reasonable and agreeable, you will make great partners in improving city policing practices.

CHAPTER 6

Establish a Hate Crime Reporting Hotline

This hotline phone number must be extensively advertised in the LGBTQ community to receive calls concerning hate crimes. If there were responding officers, how do they treat the caller/victim? In some cases, the caller would report the crime directly to the police department and this hotline to ensure our community knew about the crime. A crime report to the police is confidential, so it is unlikely the community would not know anything about it. The hotline's purpose is to help victims, monitor police behavior, and gather valuable information on hate crimes in your local area.

The person who is assigned to answer this hotline must be responsible. Their job is to take down the information, the report: victim name, address, phone, and email (whatever identifying information the victim is willing to disclose). More importantly, the caller will identify the crime, the day and time, and the location. Using any derogatory names during the assault would help to identify it as a hate crime. This may confirm that the crime is hate-motivated. Did the victim, or anyone else, call the police? Was the interaction between them and the officers positive or negative?

The telephone staff should have a simple form with blank lines to enter the victim's information and account. PERFECT! You have everything you need to take this matter to the police to report a previously unreported crime or raise the issue of police misconduct if the victim mentioned it.

If you have an LGBTQ center, you don't need a dedicated line. The center staff can answer and take the report. If you do not have a center, you need a dedicated phone line in 'someone's home and a dedicated person who will answer it. You don't want to use someone's existing phone number in case the monitor tasks switch to a different person. Remember, this phone number is widely advertised, and you cannot change it. The main caution is to ensure the monitor knows that those who call that special number may have been ignored by police or injured in the assault, and special sensitive care is needed when addressing the caller.

Advertise this hotline number on flyers and post it in all local gay and lesbian businesses, especially in bars and discos where predators often seek out their victims and assault them.

Publish this number in all the free community entertainment newspapers which often include personal ads and are placed in bars and elsewhere. You might be thinking if the number is just the general number at the local LGBTQ center, it does not need to be advertised. Oh yes, it does. People don't know that the center now offers to make reports of hate crimes. You need to advertise this new service. It can be something like, "If 'you're the victim of a hate crime, call the center at XXX-XXXX and report it there as well as to the police. We want to help and support you to make this important record of your assault."

When I monitored the hotline, I usually met with the victim and personally interviewed them face-to-face and in greater detail. I wrote about some of those assaults and murders which are included in the reference material list at the end of this book. This was important because I was not just the monitor but also the police relations liaison. I visited many victims to take their reports, usually using a tape recorder for accuracy.

Once you have some reports of hate crimes, give each report (save a copy for your files) to the individual in your FACE Task Force so they can present them personally to the appropriate police staff member. In my case, they were always given to the Chief of Police or his lieutenant. Part of the work of the FACE task force is to begin relationship-building efforts with a high-ranking police staff member with whom you can consistently work. This is huge!

Understand that assaults are the most common crimes committed in any city, so it is not shocking or special to the police when someone is punched or beaten. When they happen in the LGBTQ community, it's often a hate crime, and with enough reports, it can show a pattern. Just to be clear, if a man is beaten up outside a gay bar, it might be a "simple" assault, perhaps part of a robbery, but if the assailant calls him a faggot or uses other derogatory epithets, it shows the motivation was hate-based. So it becomes a hate crime. (More details: Ref #1 and #2)

One other comment about an important aspect of gathering hate crime reports directly. Most police departments and county governments collect hate crime information to determine if there is an increase or decrease in it and to record other trends. These data are important to track general trends. But the details of these crimes held by the police department and the county are confidential, not public information. Therefore, we cannot address any specific crime. But the hate crime data collected directly by the LGBTQ community is information you can act on right then and there and bring to the attention of the Chief of Police, other city officials, or the public, IN DETAIL. The crime reports, including details from personal interviews with victims (and/or witnesses), will make a jolting, eye-opening news article.

Hotline Summary

The LGBTQ community Hate Crime Reporting Hotline is only useful if the police are not properly doing their job and encouraging victims to report all crimes or if the community perceives police will not respect them if they do. If the police department is in full cooperation mode, then the hotline can be used slightly differently. Instead of being used to record crime reports independently, the hotline can be used in a transitional way to inform the caller that the police can NOW be trusted and that they need to report the crime directly to the police, as should be the normal procedure. You can even point out that the community and police have been working hand-in-hand to stop hate crimes. The value and use of a hotline depend on how much cooperation your city's community has with your police department. One task of the FACE Task Force is to expand that cooperation to the max, which may take a few years.

How long will you need to operate a hotline? As long as it is needed. In my case, I monitored the Hate Crime Reporting Hotline for six years. I probably could have stopped after three or four years since the police department responded exceedingly well, but I wanted these calls to the hotline to go to zero, and they did in six years, so I discontinued it.

CHAPTER 7

Approach #2
When the Chief of
Police is non-Responsive

First, understand that the Chief of police is neither self-appointed nor elected. County sheriffs are elected, but if you work in an unincorporated area of a county, you would be working with the 'Sheriff's Area Commander appointed to be in charge of your local 'sheriff's station. Many smaller cities don't establish their own city police department due to the high cost; they contract with the county for police services. So, whether you are dealing with the city Chief of Police or the County Sheriff's Area Commander, they each have bosses they must report to. So they are subject to "public pressure," which I prefer to call reason. I'll refer to both the Chief of Police and the Sherriff's Area Commander as the Chief of Police. There are several ways to get the Chief to see the light. Let me list what I think will be productive. I'll list them from what would take the least effort to the greatest effort.

The City Council hires the Chief of Police (and writes county police service contracts), but the City Managers administer the city. Before meeting with the City Manager, hold a meeting with your FACE Task Force and become familiar with the issue or issues at hand, such as gay bashing, discrimination, police brutality, or other misconduct. City officials have a fearful respect for an organized group. You're presenting your community as highly organized. One individual will have little sway, but an "organized" task force is a big deal. Plus, in many cities, which may seem odd, the LGBTQ community holds considerable respect.

Lay out your case, "We have issues with the police department… We had some recent beatings and the police are non-responsive…

We pay our taxes and we want the police department to serve and protect us too."

Be rational and calm. This direct approach *may* just solve your issue or at least be a great start by shining a light (maybe for the first time) on the need to improve community policing. The City Manager would then call in the Chief of police and require him to change his unacceptable behavior and begin to respect the call to treat residents with dignity and equal justice, or… be fired.

CHAPTER 8

Approach #3
When the City Manager is non-Responsive

The City Manager has bosses too. They are the members of the City Council. You can go to a City Council meeting. As required by state law, these meetings have time set aside for public comment. I have used this approach on occasion.

Let's say someone was beaten, the police department was non-responsive to your complaint, AND the City Manager was also of no help. You could offer your concern publicly at a City Council meeting. When you arrive at the podium, speak into the microphone, such as, "My friend was assaulted while leaving a gay bar. We called the police, but the officer who arrived would not take a report." Sometimes I "play dumb." I raise the issue politely as if I am confused about the problem, so I am not blaming anyone. I can tell you that getting angry can be counter-productive. You might be seen as a political troublemaker instead of a justifiably concerned citizen.

Please understand, of all the officials I have mentioned, that members of the City Council are the only ones elected, and they want to be re-elected. Getting their attention is easy and huge. Do you know who routinely attends all City Council meetings? Of course, the City Manager and the Chief of Police participate in every meeting. But who else? The members of the public and, even more important, newspaper reporters will be there. Every city has something like a "City Council Beat" reporter looking for an unusual and emotional story. You can't get more emotional than talking about a particular gay bashing and a non-responsive police department. Even people who feel "gay" is not right will never condone brutal assaults and police misconduct. Elected officials break into a drippy sweat when someone publicly raises an emotional and often racial issue like this.

Let me tell you exactly what will happen in 90% of the cases. The City Council will discuss this seriously, then turn to the Chief of Police and ask him about the specific case. "Sorry, Madam Mayor, this has not been brought to my attention," the Chief may reply. Then the City Council will unanimously ask him to look into the matter and report back. The public is listening to the issue and the press is writing it down. From this point on, your expressed concern will not be brushed aside. You just made it a public matter.

The City Manager (or the mayor) will call the Chief of Police into their office, looking directly into his eyes, and will require a resolution to this particular case. Believe me; it will happen. If more than one case of police misbehavior comes to light within a short period, the City Manager, pressured by the City Council or not, might call for a review of policing policies regarding the LGBTQ community.

If a news reporter does not cover the City Council meeting, you or someone else on your task force must write that article, submit it to the newspaper, or post it on the internet on a proper website or media platform. I have written dozens of articles reporting gay bashings and even murders. It is extremely helpful to get the public's attention to bring pressure to eliminate police misconduct.

The FACE Task Force springs into action. It plans out the steps it can take, which members will take on different parts of the plan, who will speak, and who will attend meetings, and so on.

It is also common to work with allies or potential allies where ever you find them. Most City Councils are composed of five members. Maybe the council as a whole is not sympathetic to your issue, but one member seems approachable. Work with that one member and build a working relationship. As you might know, council members often engage in trading support favors, a process known as "log rolling." For example, council member A supports council member B's issue, and council member B, in exchange, supports council member A's issue. Usually, this procedure involves only non-controversial matters where there is a simple difference of opinion. And LGBTQ rights, Black rights, Jewish rights, etc., should be non-controversial, a no-brainer, as they say. If so, now you have the support of two council members, and you only need one more to pass a measure. It takes patience, strategy, and determination, but it is not impossible.

Plus, and this is a big plus, once the FACE Task Force is seen in action and winning over important city officials, it becomes more and more respected and powerful. We need to build a consensus. City Councils are the local lawmakers. They are the ultimate target of our attention. If going directly to the Chief of Police works, then that is the easiest and best plan of action. If not, begin to engage the members of the City Council individually. Make friends and allies.

CHAPTER 9

Approach #4
When the City Council is non-Responsive

First, it is highly unlikely that the entire five-member council is against LGBTQ equality. Often some members are liberal and supportive, others are conservative and not supportive but don't discount that some members simply don't know or understand the LGBTQ community. Reasonable people can be educated, and such was the case in the City of Long Beach back in the 1970s. OK, so now what? We roll up our sleeves (again) and get to work.

1. Meet individually with the members who support you and ask for their help.

2. Meet with the council members who are opposed to your position and, in a polite, diplomatic way, discuss the anti-gay violence that's going on in your community. Don't rule them out.

3. Meet with the members who just don't know and are unsure of their position on LGBTQ rights. If they are conservatives, perhaps they only follow conservative news, such as Fox News, and are unaware of the facts.

These meetings with each council person are a job for your FACE Task Force. Again, two or three task force members should attend and calmly discuss actual assault cases and actual police misconduct. Remember, ultimately, truth wins out.

4. Hopefully, you've been writing articles in the gay press that address and inform the LGBTQ community. Now it's time to write news articles in the straight press as well. Let the city at large know what is going on. Interview victims of bloody assaults. Use print media and social media to fully expose the horrible violence and even deaths that have recently occurred. Develop a website, FaceBook page, Twitter account, blog, and other media platforms,

and be sure to include the name of your city in the titles. Always expand your messages using hashtags, such as #gaybashing, #anti-gayviolence, #LGBTQviolence, #policemisconduct, #(your city)policemisconduct, and so on. Educate the straight community because, until they read your accounts of gay bashings, they will remain uninformed and tuned out on this issue. Tune them in and educate them on how dangerous it can be walking in the gay business district of your city or even in the vicinity of one gay bar.

A brief TikTok video of a gay man or woman talking about their unprovoked attack is amazingly powerful!

If your task force is doing half its job, you will bring a potent and persuasive force to your call for social justice, which no city official can ignore. Remember, they all want to keep their jobs.

5. The City Council chamber is one important forum to raise LGBTQ equality issues, but it's a forum you cannot control. Have your LGBTQ center (if you have one) or the task force hold widely advertised community meetings to discuss LGBTQ violence. Focus the meeting on a recent beating, stabbing, or murder. Post notices everywhere in the gay community. Most importantly, invite the police command staff. I assure you they will attend. (The next chapter discusses this further.)

All that I state here about the important tactics to advance LGBTQ equality can also be applied by all other minority groups. You may have to educate the members of the City Council so they will personally understand the extent of the violence your community is suffering. It takes patience, but it's most often done. In the event it is not, you'll have to vote them out of the office and elect new council members who are sympathetic to your cause.

CHAPTER 10

Approach #5
Community Meetings

I want to talk about community meetings by giving the details of the first public meeting I attended. It lit the fire in me and ignited a new focus in my life: to help stop hate crimes. (The names used here are incorrect, but the people and events are true.)

Sally Rivers, Chairwoman of the Board of Directors of The Center, opened the meeting with, "I want to welcome all of you to this special meeting with Long Beach Police." Interestingly, women have always played a significant role in the pursuit of lesbian and gay equality. "Besides having detectives from LBPD here, we have a special guest, Tommy Stavers. I'm just going to let him speak for himself."

Tommy stepped to the front center of the hall. He was a nice-looking Caucasian man with light brown hair, around twenty-five years old, tall, and with a thin build. He wore a long-sleeve plaid shirt and 501 Levi jeans, which were then the most popular attire of gay men.

"Six days ago, I was at the Hangout." He spoke clearly and showed no signs of nervousness. "I had been there for a few hours, relaxing and having drinks. It was getting late, and I thought about heading home when a guy approached me and started chatting. He placed his hand on my knee, so I put my hand on his hand. He was my age and attractive, and I loved the dimples he flashed when he smiled. It was only about ten minutes into our conversation when he asked me the questions.

"'I'm only in town for a couple of days,' he told me. He said he was feeling lonely. And then said something like, 'I have to tell you, you're the sexiest guy in this joint. You wanna connect? My hotel is kind of far. Do you live nearby?' Wow! Did I just luck out or what?! I figured he was so sweet. I told him I did and invited him over to my apartment. I live only three blocks away, and I walk to the Hangout whenever I go there because I don't want to drink and drive. So, we got in his car and went to my place. He was so nice and friendly."

The entire hall was silent. Everyone was eager to hear Tommy's story. He continued, "So, when I unlocked my door, we entered, and he immediately began to look around. 'You live here alone?' I told him yes. Then, Sam, that's what he said his name was, reached behind him and pulled out a hunting knife. My face dropped. I was in shock. I didn't know if I should run or grab something and try to defend myself. He was standing between the entrance door and me. He made a few stabs at me, cutting my shoulder. It's strange. I didn't even think about being cut. My only focus was on avoiding further contact with the knife.

"'You goddamn faggot,' he said as he swung the blade at me again. 'You fuck homo. How many little boys have you raped today?' I tried to maneuver past him toward the door. I had a small dining room table, no more than three feet wide, that he continuously lunged across to get at me on the other side. I tried to grab his arm to stop him, but he stabbed me again, this time on my left side. Then, he swung the knife horizontally, attempting to cut my face. I was finally able to take hold of his arm and pull him across the table. Since his body was in motion heading toward me, I had the advantage. I grabbed him and pulled him over the table toward me and onto the kitchen floor. He kind of landed on his head. That was my opportunity to make a run for it." Tommy paused.

"Where did you go? Did he follow you?" a man near the front row asked.

"To be honest, I didn't look back. I just ran. Maybe a couple of blocks. A couple of guys were on their front porch, probably just getting home from the bars. As I approached, I yelled, 'Help, call the police.' They took me into their house. I finally looked down at myself. I didn't realize how badly I was cut."

At that point, Tommy was quite emotional and shaking. Sally went up to him and hugged him dearly.

Then Sally invited Commander Cooper to address the group.

He began, "We appreciate Mr. Stavers filing a complaint of this incident, and we are–"

"You guys don't ever take gay-bashing violence seriously," a man angrily shouted. "We call the police when we are beaten up, and you guys don't even take reports, you–"

"Hold on, please," Sally interrupted the interrupter. "You will all get time."

But the young man continued. "A friend of mine was beaten up when he left Sam's Place, that bar on Broadway. He was followed by four guys who beat the crap out of him. The police were called. I was there when they finally arrived. They refused to take a report. One officer had a smirk on his face as if it was all a big joke. He implied that my friend probably started it."

I just sat there, amazed at what I was hearing and seeing. Were the police this bad? Were they derelict in their duty to serve and protect? Were they this outright prejudiced against gay people? Wow! Amazing. Then I thought about these crimes. It's one thing to read about assaults against gay people in the gay press or hear about them by word-of-mouth, but to see a victim talk about his attempted murder is quite another. The group was not so quiet now. A lot of anger was expressed. My eyes and soul were open to all this anger and hostility. I sat there quietly, absorbing everything.

Sally raised her hands and calmly spoke. "Yes, we have grievances. We are angry. We have every right to be, but let's hear what the officers have to say. After all, we invited them here to address our concerns."

"Thank you, Ms. Rivers." Commander Cooper began again. "I know there are issues. I know we do not do everything right, but let me speak about the assault that Mr. Stavers brought to our attention. We consider this crime urgent: not just because a man was nearly killed but because he seems to be at least the third man attacked with a knife in the last ten weeks. The other two were killed, and we are investigating another homicide, also by stabbing. It happened in the same area, so Mr. Stavers might be the fourth victim of a possible single assailant." The commander cleared his throat. "I want to bring homicide detective Lance up here to discuss some details."

I was stunned. Three gay men died due to hate. What crimes did they commit? The crime of being gay? What was happening to the world? I don't like how you look, so I'll kill you? I don't like the country you come from, so I'll kill you? I don't like who you sleep with, so I'll kill you? Insanity! I couldn't just sit there and take it as some distant story on the evening news. I realized I had to do something. I had to fight this insanity, this inhumanity.

The detective stepped forward. "We have a dedicated team working these assaults," he told us. "We are investigating them as a single case. Now, there are certain details I cannot release, but the clear description given to us by Mr. Stavers is a tremendous break since all the other victims died. Associates of the other victims have given collaborating accounts of those assaults, which established a creditable MO (meaning modus operandi, or mode of operating). We have enough information to establish that it is the same assailant in all three cases and likely the same in the fourth case." The detective opened a folder he was holding. "This assailant goes to a gay bar late at night, maybe an hour from closing. He scans the room and settles on someone in their twenties who seems alone and maybe drunk. A victim alone and inebriated would be a safer victim to attack. He then displays a sexual interest and suggests they go to the victim's home to have sex."

"What is the likelihood you'll catch this guy?" an older man asked.

"Our homicide division has a ninety-percent success rate on apprehending murderers." The detective looked straight into the eyes of the questioner. "We'll get him."

Yes, we'll get him, I thought to myself, and I'm going to help.

CHAPTER 11

Approach #6
Civilian patrols

Perhaps the most impressive development created by our task force was the Long Beach Teams Project, a civilian patrol organization comprised of members of the LGBTQ community. This project came together because late-night attacks continued despite more help from the police. Other gay-populated areas in California also implemented these self-defense groups, such as Silverlake, West Hollywood, and San Francisco. Similar groups were operating in cities in other states, such as Houston, Dallas, Kansas City, and New York City.

The Long Beach patrol was unique in that it was created as a nonprofit corporation that carried liability insurance for its volunteers and had the support of the police department.

The Teams Project patrolled three areas of the city where there was a concentration of gay and lesbian frequented businesses, but the Broadway Avenue corridor, which was the longest at about one mile in length, was the most significant since the most anti-gay crime happened there. It is this team I would join most often. Our teams used walkie-talkies, cellular phones, megaphones, bright vests, and whistles as our only weapons to stop attacks. The use of a roving LBPD car gave the operation a broader view of what was happening in each group's patrol area.

Each patrol group had a team leader and five to six members to walk the corridors between 9 pm and 2 am each Friday and Saturday night. Using our cell phones, we kept in contact with the roving police car for backup if needed. (We had some of the first police-provided cell phones from the early 1980s.) Our team leader had the direct phone number of the Watch Commander on duty. Our task was to continuously walk in a group from one end of our assigned corridor to the other and back again. We occasionally saw small groups of young men, usually two or three, seemingly up to no good. We would always approach them and, from a distance, yell out, "What are you guys up to?" Most often, these men or teens were surprised and stunned to see us observing them. "We are in contact with Long Beach Police; please leave the area," the team leader would blast into the bull horn. Part of our "authoritative look" included our vest uniforms and our bullhorn. These tended to have troublemakers think twice. Of course, if the young men were engaged in normal activities, there was no issue, and we would move along.

While we patrolled these gay-frequented corridors, no violence ever took place, but we felt that we stopped a great deal of violence from happening. Do the gay-business districts in your city need a civilian patrol? It depends on the extent of assaults in the area and on whether or not the police are effective in stopping them. If the assaults increase or just persist, it's time to organize civilian patrols. In addition to stopping hate crimes, the Teams Project patrol can give the LGBTQ community great publicity, generating more awareness and action by the police. (More details: Ref #2)

CHAPTER 12

Approach #7
What If Nothing Works

It would be unusual if nothing worked. Usually, this kind of work will lead to some gain in equality, as small as it may be. Still, there are smaller towns and cities where the majority of residents believe that LGBTQ people choose their "wicked" lifestyle and only want to molest their children. They view our community as despicable, immoral, and undeserving of any legal rights or protections for housing, work, and freedoms. As my mother would say, "You're talking to a wall."

In those municipalities, discrimination lawsuits can and should be brought against the individuals and municipalities who violate federal law. However, I suggest you leave these massive legal challenges to national civil rights organizations, such as the ACLU (American Civil Liberties Union).

You may choose to leave the city that rejects your lifestyle and move to one that welcomes the LGBTQ community, where you can live, work, vote, and love freely, where you can establish a family of friends who will respect and appreciate you.

So, your work to attain equality and social justice is over.

REALLY? NO WAY! Now a different phase of your efforts begins. You must VOTE! VOTE! VOTE! Vote in EVERY election. Vote for every local and state measure that promotes LGBTQ equality and protects and expands our rights and the right of all minority groups. Vote for every candidate who seeks LGBTQ equality and protects and expands our rights and the right of all minority groups. This includes judges, a mostly ignored office.

Of course, most of you have always voted. Thank you. But you must double your efforts, reach out to others you know, and plead with them to vote.

Choosing LGBTQ favorable candidates is usually an obvious choice. Just listen to their positions and the positions of their political party. How do you know what measures are pro-LGBTQ? Often, the titles of these measures are deceiving and the text is confusing. How do you pick judges that will advance our rights and the rights of all minority groups?

In major cities in all states, there are political groups of LGBTQ people who come together and work diligently to examine proposed measures and the positions of the judges. A little internet searching will bring them up. Take their recommendations and VOTE, VOTE, VOTE!

CHAPTER 13

Approach #8
Police Complaint Commission

In addition to voting non-cooperating council members out of office, there is an additional approach you can take directly to reform the police department in your city. In some cities, police misconduct is pervasive and seemingly a part of the police brotherhood culture. Clearly, in some cities, in some circumstances, abusive police officers are not stopped or punished by their command staff often because the command staff never hears about this bad conduct. Such was true in LBPD between 1960 to 1990. The city council could have created this civilian board or commission to oversee internal police misconduct procedures. However, the city council was not willing, likely due to the political influence of the police officers' union.

Therefore, in 1990, the citizens of Long Beach submitted a ballot measure that would create a civilian board of review. This extraordinary measure passed and created the Citizen Police Complaint Commission (CPCC). Citizen complaints of police misconduct could no longer be swept under the rug.

The CPCC has the authority to receive, administer and investigate, through an independent investigator, allegations of police misconduct with emphasis on excessive force, false arrest, and complaints with racial or sexual overtones.

The CPCC is neither an advocate for the complainant nor the police personnel. Their findings can result in the accused person being disciplined, trained, or exonerated. The Commission cannot, however, recommend the type or extent of discipline or penalty. While the Commission does not set policy, its findings have resulted in policies being changed or clarified to best serve the community.

While some community leaders wanted a commission with more teeth, this was a middle-ground solution and one that works well. If your city council is unwilling to create such a civilian review board, contact the City of Long Beach and other larger cities that have established a civilian review process for police complaints and learn how they achieved it. Create a ballot measure in your cities to do something similar.

Conclusions

Whether you are a small group or an individual who musters up a few others, come together and approach the issue of expanding LGBTQ rights and the rights of all minority groups. Form a task force, discuss and develop a strategy. Brainstorm and take on the issues one by one, step-by-step. You may come up with additional approaches, and that's great, but patience, diplomacy, determination, and constant effort are what is needed. Finally, always vote and help promote measures and candidates who embrace our goal of equality.

Acknowledgments

I have had a fascinating life (so far) and the extraordinary privilege of serving my beloved LGBTQ community for nearly fifty years. I hope this book will help stop hate crime, not only in the LGBTQ community but in all our precious minority communities where we experience such violence.

I want to acknowledge the love,

support, and help from the following people:

Marie S. Hogan

Ken Mardian

Pat Rass

Caroline Clark

Joan Ferlisi

References

#1 *My Life on Purpose: Fending Off Death, the Catholic Church, the Aids Epidemic, and Hate Crimes*, 2022 -

This book includes:

a. The case of a young Black man, a former roommate of mine, who was brutally tortured to death.

b. The case of a gay man who was attacked at knife-point while exiting a gay bar and tried to stand up for himself.

c. The unique case of a police program called a "reverse sting operation" where police set up two young "gay looking" officer decoys to present themselves as vulnerable and see who dared to assault them.

#2 *The Chartreuse Garden: The Horrific Murders of Innocents that Compelled Me to Fight Social Injustice and Hate*, 2021 -

This book includes:

a. The case of the "gay stabber," a young man who pretended to be gay, followed guys home as they left the bar, and murdered them. An interview of the victim who survived is included.

b. The case of the apartment managers who brutally beat their tenant who had AIDS within an inch of his life. I interviewed him and hand-delivered his case to the Chief of Police, who took immediate action against the responding officer who filed a false report.

c. The case of street thugs who preyed upon gay men and continued to operate with impunity because the police refused to take reports of these crimes. This was another case I brought to the attention of the Chief of Police and worked with him to arrest this gang.

d. The case of a gay basher attacking a young Jewish man in a parking lot and beating him severely.

e. In addition, in *The Chartreuse Garden*, I explained my involvement in police training at the Long Beach Police Academy on LGBTQ issues and concerns. Lastly, I described the Long Beach Teams Project that patrolled the gay business districts. It was a group of gay and lesbian volunteers who the police department trained on how to stop a hate crime before it happened.

#3 Website - JackCastiglione.com:
Under the "Gay Right" tab, the drop-down menu:
1. Getting involved in Long Beach anti-violence work.
2. A discussion of hate crimes.
3. How the Long Beach LGBTQ community got organized to stop. hate crimes
4. Video, "Straight Hate."
5. A sample of the newspaper article written to stop hate crime.

#4 Please visit the YouTube channel, Jack's Gay Chats, for up-to-date community information.
https://youtube.com/c/jacksgaychats

About the Author

Partial history of Jack Castiglione's work in equal rights is on JackCastiglione.com

Life Interest:

Civil rights, especially LGBTQ rights, as well as equality for women and people of color.

Education:

BS Degree in Political Science, California University at Dominguez Hills, 1970

Professional Experience

Member Long Beach Chapter of Dignity, an LGBTQ rights organization to confront the Catholic Church on its unjust treatment of LGBTQ members. 1981 – 1986. Was chapter President 1984 – 1986.

Long Beach Lambda Democratic Club member and served as the Chairman of the Police Relations Committee from 1985 to 1993

Chairman of the Long Beach Police Chief's Advisory Committee representing the LGBTQ community on police abuse matters 1986 to 1992

Police Academy instructor to train police cadets on LGBTQ community issues of concern 1987 - 1993

Established the Hate Crimes Reporting Hotline and monitored it 1986 – 1992

Long Beach Teams Project, an organized and LBPD trained volunteer group to patrol gay business district street to stave off anti LGBTQ violence. 1992 - 1993

Hospital Visitation Team member, professionally trained visitor to comfort PWAs (Persons with AIDS) 1986 – 1992

Shut down a change ministry group (Beyond Rejection) in Long Beach operated by Jim Johnson under the guise of being a benevolent AIDS Hospice House, 1987

Human Rights Commissioner of the City of Long Beach 1991 - 1995

Publications

Numerous newspaper articles in the Long Beach Press-Telegram as well as in the LGBTQ press. Examples found here: https://www.jackcastiglione.com/gay-rights-articles/

PBS film "Straight Hate" features Castiglione, 1992

The Chartreuse Garden: The Horrific Murders of Innocents that Compelled Me to Fight Social Injustice and Hate, 2021

My Life on Purpose: Fending Off Death, the Catholic Church, the Aids Epidemic, and Hate Crimes, 2022

How to Stop Hate Crime: My Guide to Engage Police & City Officials to Quell the Violence, 2022

Awards

State of California, Certificate of Appreciation, Lambda Police Relations Chairman, 1990 – 1991

State of California, Certificate of Appreciation, Lambda Police Relations Chairman, 1991 - 1992

State of California, Certificate of Appreciation, Lambda Police Relations Chairman, 1992- 1993

City of Long Beach, Certificate of Appreciation, Human Relation Commission 1991 - 1993

Lambda Democratic Awards for Police Relations 1993

Congresswoman, Bette Karnette, Certificate of Appreciation, Lambda Police Relations Chairman 1993

Recipient of the Harvey Milk Foundation Award, 2022.

Testimonials:
Letter from President Obama, 2017
https://www.jackcastiglione.com/

www.ingramcontent.com/pod-product-compliance
Lightning Source LLC
Chambersburg PA
CBHW060628030426
42337CB00018B/3246